Chaotic Clarity

By Eli Childers

Disproportionate disappointment about populous popularity consignments, like just once in a millennium line up lifetime looking for a break kid, that space between hoping for the best and staying on my grind kick is where you'll still find me keeping it sunset faded bliss. The underdog danger split that indicates I haven't made it yet. But you see, when it comes to me, I always hope for the best, so until next time just wait for my "Oh My God" goodbye kiss.

The hibiscus leaves bowed under the heavy love of the storming precipitation. They waved to me in slight resignation as if to say "I'm not ready for such passion". It was a weighty love ever so unhealthy, and the beauty of growth would not be seen for several more seasons.

We all stood there in the washed out laundromat of desire; me, my heart, and my soul. It seemed that any further negotiations had reached a standstill and there was no more compromise to be made in the discussions. I backed away from the tabled points and moved toward the window in frustration. The sky outside was sad and I could tell that its gentle tears rolling out over everything had been a long time coming.

Feeling jet fuel empty with similar symptoms in the middle of an aerial tailspin hoping for the best, but seeing the ground impact approaching, so I grabbed the eject button and then kissed my past goodbye like so many parachuting assumptions.

The water of circumstances moved around me like a river birch standing firm without yet learning the meaning of big words, like courage.

The coolness of the liquid caressed the hurting torrents of storming violent surges and struck "back to square one" lightning circuits.

And so I leaned gently into the perceptive opportunity for growth and wisdom then decided that these things were well within my branch arms reach, and I should continue to seek them, I was reminded that all of my dreams were fierce birds on steady perches waiting for passing turbulence to return calmness to ruffled feathers in the sun rays of warm blessings.

The edge of the world fell over the lips of my late night cereal bowl and kissed the awkward room goodnight. The reality of responsibility and the dream of life were lock step lovers found on the opposite sides of the same coin. They were my "Tristan and Iseult" lovers, cursed to always be together and yet forever apart, torn asunder. The notion of such a romance turned my soul over in restlessness, and so I carefully ran water into the milk and turned out the kitchen light in response.

He sat as still as possible in the ambient sound of his aching heart. It was like Ella Fitzgerald singing sweetly and almost inaudibly low, but he knew that she was singing right to him.

The edge of the valley was an overgrown monstrosity of wire connection vines run from unknown places going unknown directions. It was the thickest part of the modern jungle, and feeling he could go no further he released the heavy backpack of life. It fell from around his shoulders and landed with a thud. He sat down on the leaf littered floor of broken dreams. Defeat was in the air and he could feel himself giving into the exhaustion. He called out in a frustrated voice to anyone who would listen, and the universe responded in a sliver of pink magenta sunlight erupting into existence far beyond the chaos. The very sight of such beauty gave him encouragement to continue on, and so machete in hand he ventured into the wilderness of the day, mostly ready.

I sat there in the coffee shop completely transfixed with overwhelming emotion. My eyes ran across the parking lot for help, but found only worried day dreams. The song that was playing overhead pulled me back in and rolled along my soul like a tractor digging large trenches that had previously been re graded by the busyness of everyday events. I knew that there was special care to be given to my steps. The field of my heart was undergoing reconstruction and the sink holes of possibility were like an abysmal renaissance period; on one side the dark ages and the other, pure enlightenment.

Her eyes stood in the rain vacant like church on a Monday afternoon. She expressed a regretful longing that my mouth had no comfort for, and my hands knew all too well the worded cure, but I refrained from speech. We both looked back as if knowing the thoughts of the other, it was considered to be a true hour designed by fate's irreverent fury. The dull pain was only eased by the encouragement of time passing further.

The long legged affluent young women walked out of the bathroom unaware of the dragging toilet paper stuck to the bottom of what must've been very overpriced booty boots. I sat there in the booth of my birthday breakfast both embarrassed and amused by the scene, and I thought redundantly "wow, isn't that just a metaphor for life."

I sat down in the VIP amphitheater seats to watch my emotions duel it out in this winner take all playing for keeps, so I nodded to each of them respectively, and then waited anxiously the whole ten paced steps of heart racing drum beats before the turn and pull gun fire release.

You stopped me right there,
I was just about to walk through those talking double doors,
It was a general sense of myself unsure,
Like, if I go this far there's no hope for return,
let alone cure,
I held the moment for a time period obscure,
And then I continued on into my new life, reborn.

These grand ideas are going round tabled conference, with knights of virtuous intent, talking nonsense in circles of disproportionate consignment. You know? The 80/20 split, bereavement pit of the stomach basement just waiting for the first opportunity casement of super hero capes sent coming to save these subtle hints of blessings still at the hilt of dagger shanks. The chipped flints of obsidian reflected dents too numerous for ordinary repeated prints.

He climbed the large oak tree positioned lonely in the backyard of his heart. It had sat stoically for more than 12 months with little more given to it than a passing thought. Today though, today he ascended the heights of its aging bark with a new notion. Today he had decided that no matter the hurts and no matter the scars, that he would fly from its twisted branches and return ready for a brand new start.

I see you there with your aspartame brain going process strain as if the metaphorical game was set to level tame and you didn't know conceptually that you're stuck in a prepackaged cage far removed from a needed free range, so I suggest you call in sick a few days and study up on necessary claims, that is if the threshold for pain isn't more than the desire for change.

He walked out onto the bow of the ship. It was a place where heaven and earth met for one last kiss, and instantly with encourage bliss a billion spectator stars gathered for what was sure to be a final parting glimpse.

He woke up among the forgotten jungle of passed up opportunity almost a little too late, the humidity seared the air on both sides with high arched polarity gates, and in a hurried anxiety mind state he did his best try at orchestrated planned escape. The tiger trapping tank he had quick sand sank was the kind of comfortable quaint he had only ever read of. It was sharpened with modern society planks of ready, set, now ok break, and so he named this place on his new world adventure traipse, the place of "Unnecessary Length" or "Apathy Lake". It was marked with a sign that read, "a souls quick death fate, now turn away."

His mind played Russian roulette with the idea of change. It was an increasingly deadly game and with one word the possibility wasn't so much brave as it was borderline insane. He looked deadpan into adversity's face and whispered, "What's my name?"

The painted concrete floor was irregularly patterned to reflect the rustic theme of the small town dinner. It was a faux misconception that made the whole scene much less realistic than he thought was anticipated. It reminded him that often we are placed in likewise circumstances, and in order to be our truest self we must go against the grain of predisposed design romantic.

I sat tepid at the red checkered tablecloth dinning set. It was a half-filled room full of very self-important personalities. I could tell by the anxious looks on the scattered faces that everyone else was just as confused about the moment as I was. A bearded gentleman who ran the wardrobe chuckled in nervous banter, "there's WIFI, but I don't know the password."

Circumhorizontal arc shifted directions in technicolored displayed glyphs. It was a blessed small consolation start to the necessary newness of beginners set your marks. I thought to myself, "I'll take it in the no nonsense mindset of never forsaken part trips."

Swaying winds greet the trees as a distant friend, returned unannounced from faraway lands, it comes in close again and then shakes the hands before returning once more, to where it began.

The peach colors rose and fell in magenta story prose. It was as if the world was calling to me, saying hello. I sat idle for a stone's throw and thought how can I refuse? That was right before I stepped out of the confinement of monotone fearful pose, and then accepted that this world is what I make of it, and my thoughts determine the ultimate course.

The morning transitions between the hard line emotions of the long life night and the hopeful revelation of the morning light were always caught between blurred interpolations of what I had always assumed to be my own lack of understanding. What it meant to be wrong against the desire to always be right. It was in this place of not quite dead failing eye sight, and not fully alive full price photo pride where awareness finally set in, that truth of it's not always a take it in stride continual fight, it was here that I realized there is no real need for a position other than that of I'm going to be more than alright, in fact in due time I will shine among the heavens on the other side of circumstantial hype, and when I arrive just know, I will shine for you, and you too will be just fine.

You run this way and that way in sparking newness heat of inward stars with synapses fire repeat. When I lay down you are with me going over and over in stark paper seedling trees, suggesting I get up from my needed sleep, and create some form of reality soul faucet leak. You are always with me and though I welcome you with open arms I cannot help but feel the resentful stings from other hopeful beings that see you as some sort of threat to their flowering dreams, at least that's how it seems, so I hold you close and keep you from the chains of expected slings, and just know that together we will eventually be free.

The warmth of the yellow light played tag with the irreversible memories that kept me up throughout the night, I could hear it shout, "You're it!" with playful affectionate bite. As the encroachment of colors reached my mind like a long lost lover; I felt like this was just the beginning of something better to be discovered in due time.

I have no idea what I'm doing in the constant spinning wool worth warning, the dream catcher looming of ideals running wild truant, see it's the lingering abandonment of feelings that keep telling me there's more in the coin tossed well-wishing with hard work backing that's left to be new world visited, but where I am now, is little kid can kicking with a side dish of always looking for something other than outsider among outcast who cannot find warm welcome come in. I could shout from the roof top but that feels too much like desperation.

He ran the open roads of a weary soul. His path led him toward empathetic shores off of the chosen course always beguiled by outward shows of force. It was the truth of consolidated realization wars which kept him ever ambitious beyond any worldly hold malicious. He was going to set his heart on the stars and fly into wanted bliss. Whatever the cost was it was ever gifting.

Someone help us from this cage locking Socratic rat trapping that even Socrates himself could not help, let alone understand. The feeling double multiplier times court trials under one ruling dialed, the apathy chemicals suppliers with no stance stand amplifiers, and who we all subscribe to, yet never attempt to see through to the justice side of event transpire. Well, I say, "DOWN with the shame filled liars" who spit out words that hurt in order to lift themselves higher, down with the broken system held together with duct tape pliers getting fat off of the backs of hopeful dreams constantly stuck in the quagmire of repetitive choirs, because it's the same song and dance half tired, but you've only got one life, so what are you going to do with it? I suggest you be your own boss, and then see who's hiring.

The exposed tree limbs brought on by the changing seasons resembled the shift in the very exposed way that I felt. The way I felt about things and expectations beyond my control. It was as if the world could see my very soul and the uncomfortable nature of the scene was too sudden of a place in which to be vulnerable. I decided it was time to go back home.

The mind of raw material which ate up fantastic concepts in dishes of nutritious breakfast conspiracies, then translates corresponding energy to the body miracle which dreams in portions spiritual, and then relates to the world and those in it along the same lines deeper than satirical.

Daily shoplifts of intended given gifts has rising sun temps more than just hydrogen burning blimps. All of those Hindenburg stalemate fits are up like red eye sauced cocktail shrimps, half eaten on the passing tray of opportunity missed, so go out there like morning stars sent and give your best bet with jail house bars bent, and then never take for granted anything that resembles green grass fenced.

Carnivorous omnipresent propulsion succubus, that is the knock down get back up again pirate ships, the narrow miss navigation blitz through canyon rifts with continual cannon blasts, withstanding all of life's hard knock no edit movie clips, moving in slow motion colored prints and displayed in the heart of hearts, no preparation conditioning.

This second wind winning patent pending face forward life grinning has my hustle more than just surface calm tension. No, it has my whole soul suspended over canyons of possible failure amended at the rate of a million to one ratio careening seconds per minute. It has me on better than original point of no return new life teaming, and to sit idle in empty theaters of full length horizon future hinting would be a disservice to my truest necessitated nature tremendous. In other words, a full length dissertation in an unknown dead language written.

The radiant energy was like embassy calligraphy flying feather freed above all of the local combined catastrophe we daily eat like meals from the malnutrition trees of our most bitter reprimand dining room table center piece. A repulsive arrangement of vassal decrees called out over loud speakers during the track meet of life that everyone is running, yet going nowhere in apparent hyper speed. The face palmed continual "good grief."

Resolved lull in expectation pause that keeps evolving into round table talks, and it's like we don't even know what we are looking for in our truest self-casting call. The all evening masquerading ball that no one is really ready for, but this isn't a dress rehearsal seasonal formal fall into formation stall segmented by too much alcohol. This isn't passive movements pressed between the "I can't help it" ropes and the "I can't make it" wall. This is real life in personal city hall, and this is my mental awareness hand in hand with my heart, taking a personal, walking tall.

The call gripped the room in cardiac arrest. He grabbed his heaving chest to make sure he was still present. Unfortunately he was, and through the intercom the interest accruable threats swarmed in like hornet shaken nests. From all outward appearances the only visible signs of the perceived danger was the increase in quickened breath. Other than him, the only other person there was the toddler who sat there watching "Dragon land" with small dog in hand. She had no more additional awareness than hopeful award contestants. He silently hung up the phone and asked her if she'd like a cookie break. They left that day and all of his intentions were bent on one word. Rest.

Hold your breath through the pressure air lock in slumber patterns, ready and willing from the two step dancing across unsupported bottom dropped tile ceilings with no real value apart from the 2 Cent half shillings, thrown under capital horse and cart double dealings, when we cannot part with things in the nature of all things unwilling, but I guess that's what you deal with when dealing with life and subsequent feelings.

He sat there roughed into the group of friends. He was hidden among the table conversation like distant planetary alignment waiting on scientific enlightenment. The observation deck seemed more than sufficient for a clear night of star gazing.

He messaged the stranger and posed a pivotal necessary question. The Paul Revere traitor. It was one that hinged all of existence in one single verse, tapered. He didn't expect any real answer, but it was more like his own acknowledgement of what he felt in soul fashioned moon craters. His own heart knew the undeniable truth. No matter how much he hated it, he could no longer stand the smoke and mirror players that had become the very personification of clown soothsayers caught in irreverent nominal layers. The "talk about it laters" was more like mystery capers that literally said I will lie to you now in order to save face later. He waded through the emotional vapors.

She messaged him in complete disregard and total ignorance of the situation at hand. Her simple quid pro quo conversation was tiring and he realized that she no more understood him now than she did years ago. Her leading words were only a mirror reflection of what she had hoped for in her own life. He didn't respond and chose to let his silence do the talking.

Devil's advocate playing in house hiding nooks, the simple town clothes line hook with all your bags packed then hung into pressed down into bundle piles shook like manageable carry on pocket books, all of those stick up wallets being took, like "please don't shoot", you know the inner conscious democracy crooks, that keep what should be happening on the back burner of range top hopeful cooks, and we all sit in oblivious far off distant looks once removed from actions pushed.

Purple rays through double pane window glaze. The good looking out glass distortion shade cast too late with seized minute fade, stories we cannot afford to waste, the second hand ticking gentle wave countdown to come around end of days.

He had been here before and was very aware of the feeling. It was like walking a steel I-Beam half attached to a high rise tower still in construction. The lanyard connection of his missing harness strayed wildly in the 35 mph sheer winds of indecision. He looked back only to accept that fate had once again encouraged his heart and soul to leave the complacent and stable structure and venture into the unknown. He was to assume wings of golden leaf purpose, and his soul was destined to fly. This was his chance, this was his moment, and as he shed his fear he stretched an uneasy foot over the side, looked up, and proceeded fall forward.

He slowly walked the sharp curves of his mindful truths. He did this in every passing amplitude, and was always careful of overzealous careening thought beggar's loot. The implied fear of impending idealism almost certainly indicated self-collision doom. He found that in occasionally sipping all of those clear lapis blue original views through understood basket looms, that he could better understand the rest of evolving interactive cues.

The conversation was poised upon the brink just shy of breaking. He could see that this was a defining moment in the grand scheme of all relations, and with none left to be wasted he delved into the prime number revelation; held the moment for a second, then served the notice of eviction papers.

He fell forward in pyroclastic rushing motion that upended any thought of future escape. It was a hopeless city state that lacked only the idealistic notion of additional possibility, and as the end neared the only thing left to do was welcome this new reality with open arms.

The bare chest appeared only mildly bruised from the centripetal force of loose arrogant words. They were hurled in a way similar to a hospital patient overcome with violent food poisoning. He backed up in defense. After having just taken a swift punch under rib number seven he knew that this was not going to be a fair fight. As he regained his footing he looked directly at the haughty assailant and smile as if to say, "is that all you've got?" Partner.

The porcelain bath tub full of barometric pressure raised red flag warnings along the edges of his heart that could be seen dotting the atmosphere every fourth or fifth sand dune. The sea oats signaled in a conspicuous S.O.S message. It was later translated in his mind to be one just word. Run.

The doorbell broke up the routine of the running dog and quick conversation phone calls. The voice from behind the fenestration was stressed, "My grandpa fell, can you come quickly?" Without question he let go of any prior activity, rounded up the three year old companion, threw the dog in the kennel, and bolted out the door ready.

He sat there and wrote down all of the memorable vacancies that had left ample room in the townhouse of his soul. As he categorized them in order from simple to complex, yet he couldn't help but to feel the expression of sadness come across his outwardly happy face. It was clear that the darkening storm deep in the horizon left him appreciating all of the experiences much more than one could ever expect. Each falling rain drop insisted on being known as an individual, and he could feel his heart speaking clearly and often with words like "respect" and "time."

He experienced the new morning like honeycombed surprise offering. The very inspiration of possibility burst into view half solved and incomplete like a Rubik's cube. It was a refreshing drink. Life had become a pennywise wishing well, and was ready for unashamed dreamers. In this way, he felt as if the curtains of his soul had been pulled back and the first light of a radiant star was approaching from a universe on the eve of conception. This moment had a quality best described as a loving mystery without doubts.

He walked out from the safety of the shore into the mystery of the hazy world. It was shrouded by morning fog, and from far off behind the cloud curtains he sensed completion. The coolness of the bay mudflat gripped his feet in wanted purgatory as if to say, "You're not done with each step yet." He must've walked a mile with his heart in hand before he realized he had no idea where he was, or where he was going. His only consolation was the occasional drift wood companion who encouraged him with words like, "keep at it, they're waiting, and you're going to be ok, I know it."

The day was extended by several hours in a most unpleasant manner. The process was of less than delicate procedure which involved repetitious events of the sorted variety. It was only in retrospect that he realized that in order to break the monotonous cycle of heartache he must travel not back across common space, but forward in time. He felt as if a part of himself would miss the comfortable silence associated with a soul hanging onto tragedy. It was decidedly worth the risk.

The alarming nature of the orange yellow words burned across the frontal cortex of his immediate environment. She uttered them from her lips with ease, but they were kerosene seagulls searching for a home from hurricane flight. They lighted on his heart, and with each new exclamation he withdrew further into the wild country of his own need for freedom.

He found it difficult to stay any longer than the already traversed conversation. There were several cosmetically placed words that indicated a deeper truth that was not ready to surface. The acceptance of the halfhearted banter only made it easier for him to move on with far lesser disappointment from the unfulfilled expectation. He struck quickly to end the feeling and as he did he thought to himself, "Such is the nature of lonely."

Your thermal envelope is in need of help. It's conditioned space is far beyond the measure of simple grace that's needed to accommodate my helping plate, in fact I believe in regards to all that misplaced hate that continues to reverberate inside of stone wall graves marked as messenger crates, I really think that we could use a little bit more than space.

He swam alone in the ocean of his subconscious mind,
It tossed and turned him along the divided current of what's wrong and what's right,
with the rising of its metaphorical tide he felt his body would eventually give up and his soul capsize, and somewhere between this morning and last night he both died and at the same time felt more alive.

Earthen transmission sent into the outer world unlocked prisms. The interminable prisons that keep all of those deep desire star wishings where the possibility of dreams coming true are just waiting on the last hope of rescue visiting.

Walls of windows with insulated outside noises full of no named complaints taking on degradation in exponential rates. The carry off humanity claims of extended grace when all else around you is experienced opinionated hate.

Last night I dreamt my voice was being silenced. A malevolence caught me while I was speaking and poured a bucket of lava into my heart, mouth, and chest, but my brain and soul did resist, and as I rose from the burned out remaining ash of all that I was and all that meant,

I made with my hand a single gift and threw it to the wind.

The sun whispered, "Easy does it my love. The morning has just begun and already you're up, so come away with this warming light, forgetting all those unhelpful thoughts. Come with me and watch, today we will give color to this slumbering life."

It was a star crossed meeting at a small coffee shop, but the feeling would be carried with him long after the lights had burned out and the skies gone dark. The pen fell from her nearby table recklessly and unnoticed. He noticed. It was a sign to him that destiny was calling. He broke conversation with friends and softly retrieved the writing device. Eyes met in warm embrace with smiling exchange, and he felt that this one interaction may have been signifying the beginning or the end of his life. He didn't know which. Everything before it seemed hazy and everything after felt meaningless. Unfortunately he would never find out what could've transpired. With sudden onset of ever present localized interruptions no further evidence of that longing love existed.

There was common sentiment in the conversation. It was an unpleasant feeling of dissatisfaction that we both felt, and without much need for explanation we decided to part ways in a manner of speaking, similar to the guillotine removal of prideful aristocracy from functioning society. The whole scene was a messy affair to say the least.

He dawned his armor for the last time that morning. The cool of the night air rolled in from the hutch window and gave intention to the day. It was the beginning and end of all mankind and he could taste the sweetness of its finality. He grabbed his totem and placed it under their pillows; nothing more was offered. He placed little worth in the sanctification of old rituals. Today was about them. They rested peacefully and he knew it would be the last time he would experience such worldly favor. It was calm surface tension on top of irreconcilable madness. He walked out into the wild and chose not to look back.

He laid his head down on his arm. The slow steady rhythmic sounds made statements that reaffirmed the creeping exhaustion. Words that were more like incoherent sighs that only a weary soul could decipher. He closed the gates of his mind and knew this was the final push in the race he'd already been running, and so he sprinted into victory before the closing of that day's sun dial time.

Saturn in my southern sky with vermillion shine saying goodbye to that encroaching night, and those held back tries kept at bay with all of your might for most of your life, are finally free to do whatever it is and whatever they like.

Ego concentric circles masked off and painting in body buildings that are structurally shifting through the neural synapse firing of gold pan sifting and rising up through the ranks of war time general cavalry forward marching. The perception that we are more than these minor happenings will only propel the healthy consciousness into greater personal understanding and ultimate integral acceptance.

These roads all go somewhere, continuously twisting. With side assistance breaking conditions of stop and go emotional diversions leaning inward toward needed collisions, and heading into infinite connection, no need for contrition. The simple one, two, three I'm with you soul resting without wishing or guessing. This is life as measured in constant lessons.

Worlds of words set on curbs in forgetful passing of motions absurd. The hold you in air you know will hurt when everyone around you is going "got to be" first, and not just going to work,
but going at the going rate in longing search, so you bide your time in personal church, and remind yourself in certain season how it will undoubtedly look, because the things we hear and the things forsook, aren't always the same, no matter the out loud story and bound up accompanied books, so skip that cast bait hook, and never compromise your own recipe, because remember... You're not only the one eating, you're also the cook.

Super moon in sanctuary bloom,
searching the earth like a child in an empty room,
we move smooth in dancing shoes,
holding tight to understood truths,
Truth....
That all, in fluctuating proof are just waiting to be made, to be made too soon,
As viewed from above on a quiet solitary moon.

The starry eyed constellations danced in apparent abbreviation.
They weaved in and out of linear time line elation like lovers destined for the
moment of undeniable connection. Innocent fires sparked in pheromone creation.

He drank in the sunset as if it were his last. It was an involuntary and immediate response to an emotional longing for connection. Connection to the world and connection to life. He could feel the colors brush against his skin as if carried by the movement of time. This sensation may have lasted for seconds or quite possibly a thousand years. It was all an irrelevance that didn't beg evaluation.

I looked up at the cloud shelf that stood between heaven and this realm's falling rain... I felt the wind blow up against the earth and all its inward frame as if to say, "I know you, and you know my name." I closed my eyes quietly and let go of the lingering pain. I fell into oblivion and into the arms of hopeful skies, praying.

Distribution blockage,
with water front acreage,
bought and sold in the open market,
and all you can think,
"Is nothing sacred?"

Earthen island panthers siting in stoic caption,
as if they understood the coded password to unlock this worlds forgotten melodic anthem,
the sound of which could never be recreated or mastered in some frantic halfcocked action,
it was more than mere mortals could fathom let alone imagine,
it was galactic transfer in the form of kicked off beach sandals,
it was a kiss goodnight from a long lost lover.
It was twice the sum of some harmonious treasure,
it was the meaning of life, if yet all together tragic.

Credited prescriptive measures thrown over edges, untethered. The fallible pledges to vaccinated long year stretches with turn valve broken levers. It's so wrong that by the time you wake up to hear the designer answers, the end has already arrived and your left over trampled dancers are all clamoring to throw on tear gas face masks while holding onto generational organic samples.

Frustration set in like a warm blanket during a house fire in the middle of summer. Needless to say, he just felt uncomfortable. Uncomfortable in his skin and with the constant output. There was without a doubt a lack of any significant change to his desire, and yet there was a constant feeling of running in place. He tried not to compare himself to others, but seeing so many people being celebrated and successful in their passions gave him a real sense of turmoil. He was a maelstrom of solitude. "Maybe just lonely", he thought. Lately he started to wonder if he was in fact more invisible than the motionless projections of some random street performer. The man was very discouraged and felt as though there was little point in trying. He felt like giving up and resigning himself to what was "expected" as a worker bee. He didn't feel as though anyone would notice.

Sun soaked in radiant clothes, the steam from starry hosts ascended in inspiration smoke, birthing a new soul not yet cloaked in partial woes, but with inner light did it make haste to come forward and boast.

Consumptive presumptions running amuck in quiet town disruptions,
the stepped in gumption within the soul that knows no outward corruption, just
blind idealistic functions waiting for some elusive opportunity throat lumped in, to
finally stick its head up through necessary volcanic eruption.

In another world we never met, the things done and said were never stitched into existence with needled thread, at least not in the way in which we know them, story book read.

In another world I may have passed by you on the street with just the feeling that somewhere at some time we had a moment, shared.

But this is our world. The one in which we live, and in that way all I can say is that I'm thankful for what we had.

I jump ship time traveled into a world unraveled. The thin layers of harboring
sour, peeled back to reveal a soul filled with skyward towers,
all stretching to the heavens as if to say, "I'm here, I'm yours,
Even if just for this one beautiful hour."

Numeral neural nebula, sprawled into colors of orange sepia,
the brave branch chain factual, in overhead data flight catapults,
rendering all things more than imagination insight actuals.

The war paint stained the skin deep across the scarred lines in his face. These marks were the tragic stories without words. These were his final vows to his fallen family, his last rights, and they were made from the wounds of so many battles. Battles that had raged relentlessly since the invaders had set foot on peaceful lands. He drew back his bow and whispered to his last arrow, "I will see you on the other side my love." With that his fingers let go, and all of hell's fury descended on the earth in the form of righteous rain controlled.

The cacophony cataclysm exploded from the darkness into existence. With a single word power was made to not only communicate, but to go to the depths of the soul in influence. These are the beginnings of whispering new life symptoms. The makings of mechanical organic mechanisms that have ideals such as love, hope, and peaceful conditions. These are the flowering combustions of history as we now know them. The paternal patterns combining in unison to create necessary tension so that growth can make its debut aftermath intermission.

The constellation of colors from the paint splattered table mimicked the way that my heart was beating instep with my feelings; irregular and free. It was the sound of my need for connection just waking up from what can only be described as a walking deep sleep, and so I stumbled in hesitation leaps knowing that if I just stay upright and on my feet I will eventually find myself in the arms of a love so invariably healthy and sweet, yet there is no comparison for what I hoped to find in-between, that kind of incomprehensible inner peace needed last week. I held my breath felt scared and alive all in the same blink, but at least I understood that this was more than circumstantial needs. This was a summation of the current travels of me.

Calypso dreams self-sold to the highest bidder in the empty reaches of the wanting soul's mess hall. The last call corner bar continually charging taxing tolls for fair weather conversation gold, and here I am paused, still wandering around fogged thinking that I should know the meaning of it all.

I met you there in coy stares, between the inner rooms of my subconscious glares. You were the right amount of funny and just enough care, you waited in nonjudgmental form with me visible in my awkward state of "don't mess this up" scared, you showed genuine interest with self-deprecating fair, and somehow I could tell that you didn't take yourself too serious which was important to my need for easy going wares, yet as my eyes opened I realized we had never truly spoken, and this had not been timeline real, you my love were a figment of imagination, or as some would say, my dream girl snare.

Star wandering traveler with heart always clamoring. A solitary dance through the galactic netherworld looking for similar lights to hold against the darkness of forever cold. This as told in common talks of breathing in and out with intermission paused. The enigmatic story of abandoned love with definition problem solved.

The dark corridors of his heart were playing wicked shadows with the insurmountable doubts still lingering after a lifetime of still trying to answer the question as to how. He was a child like sprout on the inside of all of his prideful shouts, and the candle he had brought with him was just one whisper from flickering out, so he mustered all of his courage went forth and made his way into the furthest reaches of his self, only to find that who he had always been was more than just lost and found.

The day had long been over by the time he decided to head home. There was little comfort in the solitude of his thoughts and he didn't expect any reprieve from the old lounge chair positioned by his front room window. All he could see were the endless unanswered questions from a lifetime of unchangeable circumstances. He sighed heavy and wore the world like a loose wedding band that was one drink away from coming off.

The wind from the mountain ridge rushed up like a surrounding flood. It was the march of a thousand armed warriors standing in arms at the general's final shrine. Howling winds and raging snow flurries of his honorable pride, these were his ultimate last signs just before entering eternal light, and as the battles ceased for one solitary night, and all at once, for all of time he held the grounds together with bladed might.

She walked the broken concrete path that ran the length of the river. It was a night of celebration but her heart was heavy with inexplicable decisions. The reflection of explosions were a pale contrast to what was erupting inside of her damaged psyche. Most of that day had already been written in tear drops soaking the innocence of her loss. She fixated on her feet. She knew that if she just kept walking that eventually she would reach the edge of oblivion. It was an off chance, but a chance no less.

Mask of who we are painted vacant by battle scars. The honorable Samurai guard of knowing that what's right is often twice as hard, so we face the day once more, forever hoping that this day will be the our best chance to lay down all of our defensive swords.

Iced down slow motion caught in that in between state so patient. The constant changing transformation consisting of the same molecular composition just transition through different external temperatures. The story of us all, existing.

Cell division in all things certain, like how and why and what is behind the next corner curtain, the destiny fated flirting with healing heart hurting, the necessary played decision in all the ways that just couldn't get right working. I mean these are not things uncommon to the story of mankind written and then read in time line dialog without spoken childlike enthusiasm blurted, but these are the lives we lead, and the things in processed press we always wish were less a tale of guarded caution tests.

Up from the cold darkness deep with unshakable intention teeth, the riding waves surface breach washing over me in primordial emotional greet, my ever present lurking beast of the mind, body, and soul salt water drink, and just as soon as you see him, just as soon as your knees go weak, it's too late and you're gone in an instant eye blink.

The city is just waking up to the keep it down dreams interpreted as sing along schemes of the broken wax rings, sealed by two centuries of ruinous kings, the oligarchy council supreme team globetrotting all over your most inherent inherited needs, like if I just shut my eyes real tight in avoidance nose clean everything will go back to the way it was in the direction my positive ideals lead, unfortunately this is false hope in the form of inaction choking weeds, and even I know that gardens have to be rooted in order to properly breathe.

The voice of smart mouth dissatisfaction kept calling to me and taunting me with school yard bully anxieties mounting, as if I needed another dose of self-conscious doubting. That mockers soul fountain found somewhere in the neighborhood of laughing houses and ambition rousing, unfortunately every other lot is the same floor plan just different numerical markings so I ran to the nearest fire gathering and decided to make a stand for the sake of sanities sounding.

Woken from a mid-slumber of a cold sleeping winter to discover she's always been there waiting, that new growth earthen rebirth just before summer heated passion wording. Her flowering love of consignment warmth that's ever so parent patent pending with longing searching. The custodial sovereign heart beat cadence hearth with rhythm timing fragrant essence firstling. She's whispering, "I'm ready so come forth please."

Baths of fire breathing situation masks that storm the villages and wreak havoc on the inner city dreaming towns, the God awful sounds of rushing wings that swooped down to consume all we are, until nothing of that starry eyed dreaming child who knows there has to be more can be found, so we stand at the ready with opportunity armor, and swords of words which were formed to make war against the great dragon, that vile creature of a life conformed.

Bird of prey with wings ablaze, you swoop down from complexity traits of volcanic haze and disturb only the part of my being that cannot comprehend in the darkness of my yesterday's going rate. You are the sun to my rays and I do nothing to block the oncoming fray. I understand that in order to live I must first be awake and so I say to you, no wait, I pray, take.... Take this soul to new places of discoveries not yet made and leave this body here in the empty hole of I can't climb out, unmarked grave. Take me to the mountain on your feathers of flame. Take me to the heights of my ultimate fate, as I never return again to this place or this call come late.

I stepped out into the sogginess of wet leaves under old house shoes. It was a waiting invitation given by the clear night sky freckled with ever present glowing distant lights. Delivery was made via an easterly wind who whispered to me slow, "I'm glad you showed. Come with me, there's so much more I haven't yet told."

The sun had come up at the expected hour signaling the world to wake, but he had already been up for some time. He sat in bed and cradled his head dreading the reality of the day. The dark circles under his eyes displayed years of anxiety beyond his age. The coffee slowly ran through the filter, and as it did he couldn't help but feel like he was sinking into the cold concrete. Just as he was about to take his last breathe of air before going under a small hand grabbed his and whispered, "Good morning daddy."

He was given a dollar and told to leave. It was the moment that he lost the last shred of hope at having a real home. The illusion was gone, and the pain of brokenness was complete. He walked out of the door and swore to himself that he'd never go back there. He was only eleven.

I took my daughter to the local donut place in town this morning. The feel of contentment hung in the mild air and although I couldn't place what it was indicating it seemed to whisper something along the lines of "I am your nostalgia and best memories." The road up ahead twisted across an old bridge that hid itself among the mixed green colored trees. I reminded myself that even when the paths are sorted it's the ride that is most valuable, so I looked at Bailey smiled and told her I loved her. I meant it.

Personifications of wisdom and patience giving time and station to a kid as rebellious as ever in nature. The needed figure direction that has no distorted waiver while I sat there with not much to offer in return,...only a pad, a pen, and something like a blank sheet of paper, eagerly hoping to catch every bit of necessary information, the not only professional line drawn cables, but the personal trench accumulation worth saving. The after storm advocate who sat in my favor when it seemed like all my chips were cashed in on chopping block tables, and it was my last farewell placed on end book gables, but after all of that, all I could possibly say quite simple is thanks, but in a way that hopefully show you that I am truly thankful.

Bold ascension waiting in canvas viewing and minds filled with pallet color consumption forming modern adventure relief tensions. The standup illustrations given through paint brush renderings making moves in the creation of thought provoking soul spark drastic non-fiction. The met need for internal commissions going kitchens on fire cooking.

Relatable traveler with pictures expandable,
the real time journey only half imaginable, that is a perspective samplings of ship
sailed happenings across expansive oceans into unknown territories. Oh to be
the first steps on land marked not only victory, but through personal triumphant
trumpeting and battle scars humbling, renamed something like "New Found
Glory." These are precious few minutes that can't be wasted in second guessing
"I'm sorrys". This is life grasped and grabbed up from the earth as it's plummeting
through the unequivocal void like a tabled feast without company, so may all your
endeavors be not only memorable but a soul satisfied universal continuum.

111

A life of open hoping without judgment payable taxed coin token.
The eye see you focus of no matter what, going somewhere with positive backs packed and a car full loaded.
The example promise of beating the odds and facing the conventional mountain summit caucus with debating harvest that is sure to reap a life of abundance.

The world and all that are in it are constantly spinning and holding tight to this life living with clenched fists and teeth and closed eyes tight hoping with all hope that everything is going to be alright as the pitch is thrown in the bottom of the ninth just shy of the home game inning constant continual inward fight, but it's those companion friends like the team's biggest fans with banner flags the read don't give up, step up to the mound, step into the light, give it your all against all odds opposition hype, and when the game is over and everyone's said goodnight we will still be with you because no matter what, that's what love is like.

Optimistic and encouraging reflective prisms without filters letting the light of immense wisdom sprawl out in pure condition and then condense back into pristine star systems which go on lasting centuries upon eons. The reliving of supportive linking that not only has the mind but the very heart of steam engines thinking. It's no coincidence that value and purpose can be written on the same line with confident words assurance, because it's just a drop in the bucket when it comes to the whole chapter's intriguing fullness and for that you always have my complete attention.

Open arms hugging all these walking storms with internal battled wars raging, the calming purpose roar of chimera eagle soaring that absorbs fuse lit floating orbs and ultimately changes perspective bitter forms into granted hand held talking gentle worlds. These are characteristics of only the most reset reprised individual spirit set on courses that are forever with us and told through the very lives not only visited but gravity defying lifted.

Sat there table and chair,
mad at the world without forthright care, hurting reversing and holding back so much overwhelming things hung on saline tears, the locked in and could not share early years of a teenager that was going several directions and at the same time nowhere, and there you were with no expectation bus fare, just a loving artistic spiritual behind the scene picture of encouragement even for those like me that felt less than capable and all together unaware.

Friendship banded brothers like no other. The kind that cannot be stamped out by time if time were some irreverent fire hunter. The call up trouble rock tumbler and joy trading founders of knowing at least one person out of a hundred million has your back no matter the trial and error of life blunders.

Fractions on visible dance floor forward unmasking with first reaction characteristics noteworthy, without asking. The "hi how are you come in welcome" that is missing in most human interaction. The left out pre judgement appreciation revolving in an individual full of positive portion rations, so thank you for the sincere group inclusion.

Optimistic surrealistic chef of positive ballistic wrecks with humor out world treks across intrinsic terrain desks. The better levels of sarcastic symptom met when so much is centered on so much less. It's when standing out among the unnecessary crowded regrets creates a natural state of being more than just brick and mortar set.

Battled and embittered starters in the broken remnants of life shattered bottles forming mosaic pick up pieces that truly matter. The colorful flower catcher grown from never ending life waters in oasis summers, so much value offered in heart coffers, that weary travelers can hear the good news no matter the obstacle courses seemingly perpetual and harsher.

Pure in heart to be set apart and crowned with golden emotion righteousness among the ever growing climbing rocks. It's the example start of standard stark when kindness overcame the land and compassion hit all arrow marks. These are the qualities that keep the spirt fed among the hungry starved, and shed the brightest light among even the most ominous dark.

A compassionate mind that unravels the complication twine of curtain call spiritual unwinding signs as told through a life's ascending vine growing on multiple temporal levels always in search of the nature divine.

Ascension level event without any need for approval or consent. Just new views over horizon rising temps that lead into passageways of welcoming fates beyond any form or past or present discouragement, and so with wings spread not clipped, I say goodbye to all of those places I and once met with consuming regret, and just for the record I have no immediate plans in return to ever see again.

Pre apocalyptic, sand scripted, uncensored, like walking up to your life in the mirror and finally saying "hey I'm with you" that native tongue speech you'd been saving since the last week of who you've always known that you were with last ditch efforts tire screech, it's the realization that you are who you are no matter how much this life and this world consume or twist the truth or your table feast, so welcome the gold leaf seats of your soul with open arms, and never let any tell you that what you're doing is beyond you or your reach.

The thought dawned on me while sitting in the waiting room. It went something like this, "only you can determine the amount of sunshine as proportionate to the incoming gloom." And as the horizon sprawled in full effective color bloom I took a step back from the internal process and gave a type of thanks for the clarity of truth. It was a type of blessed gratitude with no pursuing interlude.

The sun was going down on all of those unrealistic expectations that he kept locked away deep inside the basement of his self-honored arrangement. Words and phrases such as "you're never going to make it." No longer covered his heart like a very itchy and stifling woolen blanket, this was the moment his soul had been waiting on, a secondary awakening that could never be compared to any other avenues of his creativity. This was his new truth and it was one worth saving.

From the dark places of powerful cursory waiting stasis came the beast with no name yet. It was my persona dragon waiting that said, "I will not be pushed around with tail tucked, I will face this with teeth and claws drawn ready to take back, all that was stolen from me in that cowardly signed off parchment." So I took to metaphorical skies to make an entrance surprise on all the times counted out in scheming devise, I would consume town and village alike, of presumptive lies and create a reality of my own type. One in which what I give out can never again be comprised to create a heart of compromise.

We are all lonely travelers unaware of our surroundings and hoping for the best while we sit tucked well away within our suits of pressurized containment. We are the drifting bystanders far removed from the daily happenings going on below in those great cities states of civilized other worldly haste, and so when I see you passing through my companion cocoon, I will raise a hand in salute and tip my visor in passive "how do you do?" Maybe just maybe then we will end up in the same point later in the typical ways of haphazard rendezvous.

The destination questions had never come up; let alone ever been mentioned in any kind of real format quotient. It was almost as if I had been falling in slow motion across an endless dark ocean. Obviously it was the less than proverbial road "most" taken. Asleep at the wheel was my default major, but on this day I chose to embrace my inner most core stow away and catch the next galactic boat into a new home just forming.

Small rotations inside of the empty spaces we refer to as our everyday bait and switch placements. Those double door swings we take for granted with exceptionable patience, all the while the lingering maintenance awareness that this is not a sustainable resonates through the back of the mind like stalemates.

The accumulated condensation of changes was like an uneven catch basin that didn't quite drain right. On one end was the collection of past tries and at the other a distant light of future possibilities ever so bright. I decided that grading was not only necessary but also a site sensitive project, and not one in need of rushing through all at one time.

I saw beyond the veil of this simple beating heart into the celestial gates unarmed. It was here that I lowered my guard, opened my arms, and gave myself over to forgiveness; no matter the pain and no matter how hard.

The day felt like cold pizza to the hangover of his heart. The metaphorical whiskey in dreaming had only served to validate his awareness that everything was not ok, and in order to shake off the pounding in his head he was going to have to create a new way of relating to his desires. He quickly consumed two ibuprofen of understanding and drank a full 8 oz. of anticipation before getting dressed.

God I wish I could escape this place,
To hide away till sunny day and no longer deal with these uncomfortable states,
God I wish I could escape this place,
It's easy I know it is,
I'll just walk the edge of my compromised ledge and fall until I reach the beginning of where I have nothing left,
God I wish I could escape this place,
I've done it before in running wind scorn, in water running poured, in running till my feet are blistered and sore,
God I wish I could es...
No...
Not this time...
I will stay and deal with that hurting kid that longs to feel and even if those feelings hurt at least if I am here, I know that they are real.

Collision springs with tensile wings sprung forth into original heaps and bound together into happenstance beliefs. The peace of mind treats enjoyed often in the sporadic season of our griefs.

Sticks in sentry wooded splits,
Sit across sandy bricks separated by water ways on windy days.
The drying land mass glazed by micro/macro life,
grazed.
The sight is within spirit on fire,
Ablaze,
like closing my eyes for a moment forgetting sadness, worry, or regretful shapes,
and for that second not only feeling thankful but also safe.

Vines on figs like leaves on twigs growing into what we have. A world at risk. At the very least it's what we know exists. Thrown in man's wicked twist leaving you grey and steel monolithic giant imps wrapping streets in concrete hold us quick menu digs, that lose for the people who feel better off like deep diving divided fish.....glimpsed. Ignorance is still bliss whether that's homemade cooking...around the table fed, or simple cartoon cut out clips of what you wish you had with empty hands outstretched. It just keeps you a little off grip. A little on edge. Almost like saying, "not really sure if I can handle all this shooting star guilt, gift, ...risk, uncertainty bread fits." The trouble with table top feelings is that they are not always representatives of our overcoming speech impediment ...lisp with clock endings....tic

The thread bears the loom because it saw the coming of the tide and the pull of the moon all while the weaver organizes thoughts like flowers bloom under finger print perhaps assumed, but the completed complexity of the work will all be viewable like the stars in far off afternoons.

They had come for me. Burning my house cheerfully, and my spirit blew a prayer into a pile of leaves, then off it went on a swirling breeze, and as I was pulled away towards the setting scene; I waved goodbye and for the first time wasn't me. I was released. I was free.

Pier diver off of roof top jump survival, that keeps your essence thriving in times that skin failing under fire flier is admiring clouds on bird wiring, or water logged emotion struggle sinking fall sighing   ... Driving toward cut through entrances like interjected mentioned glances of twirling dancing treatments… rehabilitation tremendous .. The sacredness of cave top mountainous arriving summits. They are steeper more than the feelings of five, seven, or six different senses. Not working independently, but all at once like no kind of stop chance ignorance. Admit it, you're tired of all the barb keep you out fencing. Well, at least that's what I hear is the functional consensus.

Cloudy hues against blue backdrop news... rain soaked agreements over tea time truce.., hold up... Put together thought patterns let loose... Car jammed traffic on loop... a life on sideline view... given the circumstances I'd say you might as well chase after your dreams… so run… don't walk...the endeavors are in pursuit.

Perched over fading jasmine was the call to ancient artifacts unearthed in complex grids of substation hanging verbs. Those highly efficient yet non confirmatory words that speak to the human state of mind... All those quietly important actions emerged.

Endurance like flowering violet green... showing urgency like spiritual flux shot out currency. The irrelevant going blurry... See? Saw playground midtown balancing beams with these objects like standing red rocks over canyon rear view earthen cleave... Those down and dirty rolled up sleeves, which gave no mean time concept of back story vowel weep. All found in pools where you ground water seeped in the shallow shoals leaked. This is real time downloadable treats. Go go go its 4am and you can't sleep in physical worn pleats. Possibly over stimulation from societal fluorescent screens that reflect back upside down and inside out of eyelid bass-drum expectation beats.

Unravel your baffled and come up off of the skinned up gravel. You laid there too long hoping to sink into the ground like pressure dug shovel. Come away from all of that internal upstream dog paddle. Don't you know this is your day to savor, this is your judgment gavel to swing out the window like a broken hammer, because whatever has happened doesn't matter? You are a new prodigal on return from a terrible travel, so come up off of that asphalt shadow, and sit at the best seated table unfettered. I'm going to tell you a story and it doesn't include any tragedy that has already left you feeling labeled. You are not your own fable. You are made for so much more than capable. You are the earth and the skyscraper, so find rest in green invited pastured with horse drawn circumstances stable.

Tears in neutral wall color covering paints,
Shed from saddened mothers and gallant martyred saints,
With warrior brothers staggered in ranks,
Defending sharp and ferocious like spears and stakes,
The righteous indignant framing planks,
Watered logged from traveled mile gates.
The hold on for goodness sake,
I'm coming for hands,
So give it a moment,
Just wait.

I looked up at the sky and put my hand in front of my eyes. I could touch the satellites, I could touch the fireflies, and I could touch the night. I held the gaze for what seemed like days and with a single voice and a single phrase I said goodbye and went inside.

The purple gray of the cloud cover was very similar to the way I felt over the terrible Kirsten Dunst movie I had just watched. It was a lingering feeling of perpetual wasted time and defeat, so I waited there hoping that the cold steel of the rain would wash the undeniable shame of my entertainment choice clean.

Your serving a mighty king, more wicked than the word wicked can describing sewing seam, as if your very heart and thoughts and hopeful dreams were subject to terrible crowning schemes, that twist the appearance of what direction contentment and pleasure lean, into corrosion leaded springs, like oily leathered wings, the very likes of which beat the air and breathing living scenes, until all the beating pouring bleeds, and what you have left are pennies on the dollar gold plated rings wrapped around "I got those needed grasping things."

Curse you oh self-betraying spirit, as if what I hear and what I feel couldn't be said clearer, the masquerade patter pitter of dancers set on replay tracks sadder, the double blind testing sample that neither sets well nor makes things composition level, oh to be that free and then to dream without the sense of constant ego figure fire fighters with nothing less than predetermined futures rising brighter instead of seeing the endless shadow storm clouds gathered. That would be bliss if bliss could be captured and measured.

I repelled down the infinite transverse parallel, into unknown territory where no man lingers and no soul dares to dwell. Unlocking open doors onto multiple landings of winding interconnected stairwells both colliding and crossing into separate halls without rhyme, reason, direction, or cause, like a soul eternal and free of worrisome cares, yet all of this is inconsequential because in the end it never was like catching unawares in loud ringing without initial iron bells.

I faced the earthen star campers in stoic silence that echoed across these reality canyons. Traveling with raw handles thrown over roof top pinnacle shambles of existence strongholds and then gave them no endless second glances like Sudoku masks that are put on faces like opaque glasses through caught up spinning trances. The cut fang lips gambles of worded anxious plans that no one will ever know as if waiting for some come round history fascist. These are the inner working of an imaginative analyst.

Musical Mephistopheles going modern day analytical obstacle advocate strengths, on floor covered mine sweeps, of unsung lyrical democracy track meets like a cut up club Ares that's had way too much fruit of the gods sacred drink. The open come see looking glass epiphany of scroll fed prophecy reciting divine soul spun vinyl urgency going nebula drive by shoot em up shopping spree, as we all sit back and watch the sun rise on another album 3rd degree. The felt up spiritual side street positive vagrancy of just what you're saying G. Holding it down like Friday pay checks at the end of long week.

I plunged head first into the outer bank ethereal plains and floated along the cooling waters of levitating leviathan lakes. The ox bow going my way that has no specific open mouthed bay and flows for miles so that it can never be tamed.

Seven angels on seven levels, who left through the gates of heaven, to find out why there were so many earthen devils, decided to stay awhile where it was less than pleasant,
and couldn't find their way back to the capital,
so they became more and more resentful,
and gave little care for the plight of any certain trouble,
and thus became the first spoken examples of hurting preamble.

Meta classic fragile fractures tragic inside of wrapped up seal tight gaskets. The Oh my goodness rings around nebula clouds like magic and rather disfigured drastic for scaled down sadness just so I can say, isn't that nice kid. You're all excited for anticipated madness that hasn't happened yet. Don't fret just keep at it.

The stranded phone lines strafed in and out through the over grown tree line like a snake on a fruitless vine with just one purpose in mind; to reach you in connection nick of time and emotionally unwind.

I walked to the precipice between you and us,
and said to myself just loud enough, that I can't go on just because.. Not for any reason as if reasons were too much,
But more for the fact that it doesn't feel like, well like I know it must . So I threw my hands to the wind, and released the held back ash and dust. And that was the last time that I spoke of love.

I wore the world like a piece of torn fabric sheet. Carefully cleaned and folded, neat.
It all fell loosely to my feet, and at every emotion crease with subtle lightning strike I told myself it was going to be over soon, that this was just reverberation spiritual exhaustion bleach. Just a moment of release.

Clouds on parade,
sustained in calm right on timing rain. No gray,
The wash away songs that cool a burning ear tongue when it's been heater
strung. The emoticon sign inward lung, functional in dual outlet prong, always
grounded to every facet of I absolutely am right where I belong.

The pull of a double planet truth as illuminated in the now night sky groups,
Like undeniable proof of the larger scale evidentiary roots within all of creation's
colorful hues. The beauty of a large scale design inside of our tiny cosmetic
ground surface level boots. It's the gravity hold you down body soothe of not
getting too carried away from what can never be understood at any given phone
booth. Just another day stuck gazing at all that we push away and hoping that
this is a moment where we finally are going say everything that needs to be
within us let loose.

I looked into the expansive solitary night with distant planets hanging in my mind like mmmmhhhmmm that's just right,
The passing by moments always closer than skin tight, and it was in this place of takeoff flight that I let go if my isolation inhibition and asked the sky to marry me to the impact of electron strike.

Bars in tempo on windows and doors,
Guns in hands of hate filled chords,
Past and future wrongs without present cure ,
all in crescendo of unforgettable songs impure.
Please don't play it again. Please don't play it again. It doesn't belong. Of this I'm sure.

Obstructive internal condition of opposition with regressive weary pilgrims on shifting road side pickings. The midnight wicked clock ticking and the day star treasure gifted. The whole grain eat up spirit lifted and the dry ground can't go on famine. The no shame rambling and the wise man offerings. When it comes down to it sometimes it's just a matter of perspective happenings in less than appealing packaging, so go ahead make the most out of every situation.

Stables of sable hair fables,
Telling tales on roof gables like stories ladled into bowls eaten in fenced in cradles. The mix up equalizer fader.

Concrete maze stated dry phrases that stunned the pace into snail crawl breaks. Like caught in snow drifts mid night late with no shelter safe. The reminder of locked gates with no sign of trace entry keyed heart shapes. Hands up, this is emotional robbery for goodness sake.

Fledgling wanting philanthropy in brain muscular atrophy,
Like thorns from rose garden structural floor canterleve,
Rrrr can you say emotional roller coaster trampoline,
Going back and forth like volcanic lava amygdala heathen teens.
It's just shelled out snap peas on dinner table palm leaves, and if you catch the meaning,
Well then I guess the average is more than what's the seaming tease.

Blurred curves of simple lures,
The come follow me assurance of what we can never cure,
The inner most beautiful hopeful words,
Spilling out in a synthetic surge of acidic lemon life mash up purée,
The no need needless to say "I'm hurt,"
"Me too,"
Tree limb perch,
Only to view celestial Andromeda lane change merger of stars and skies over lost city ruins.
The masquerade ballroom insurance,
Set in places of rice flat courage.
Better run before you've lost all similar heart and soul fly away birds,
Those necessary virtuous moments of nurturing heaven sent firsts.

I climbed up to the mouth of the eternal inner sleeping beast,
and shouted inside for at least a week.
No thunder,
No rumble,
No sounds came to me,
Just ruble in the path of memorial feast,
So I turned around tore my chest with ease,
took out my instrument of emotional peace and tossed it forward before heading
back to take my ship on to the other side of realities beach.

Don't try and stop the rushing tide,
Let it overtake you,
Let it collide,
Make mistakes,
Make amends,
Nothing is irrevocable,
Welcome to this dance we call life,
So give it another try,
Take it all in stride,
Let down your guard,
Give up your pride,

Love more,
Love longer,
Hold onto the sun,
Don't run for cover,
don't run and hide.
always and forever by your side

Last night I dreamt of all the struggles and where I'd been,
With horseback riding against the wind,
I took my place as brother, father, friend,
I took my starting with rein in hand,
Land locked mental marks,
stark and naked,
like a blemish among the sand,
From south of together, to the water, to the fields,
And then back again,
I whispered to my horse, "we will be ok. I have a plan."
Then with that and last survival adrenalin,
I closed my eyes,
Breathed deep,
And felt my dream come to an end.

Dedicated to my daughters Bailey and Iris.

Their love is a renewing spring.

The last blank pages are for you…. Good luck, and may your searching never end.